SUPER SMART
INFORMATION
STRATEGIES

TEAM UP ONLINE

by Vicki Pascaretti and Sara Wilkie

CHERRY LAKE PUBLISHING • ANN ARBOR, MICHIGAN

A NOTE TO PARENTS AND TEACHERS: Please remind your children how to stay safe online before they do the activities in this book.

CHERRY LAKE
Publishing

A NOTE TO KIDS: Always remember your safety comes first!

Published in the United States of America
by Cherry Lake Publishing
Ann Arbor, Michigan
www.cherrylakepublishing.com

Content Adviser: Gail Dickinson, PhD,
Associate Professor, Old Dominion University,
Norfolk, Virginia

Book design and illustration: The Design Lab

Photo credits: Cover, ©Eduard Stelmakh, used under license from
Shutterstock, Inc.; pages 3, 6, 13, 14, 29, and 31, ©iStockphoto.
com/bluestocking; page 4, ©iStockphoto.com/Skeezer; page 16,
©iStockphoto.com/nano; page 18, ©iStockphoto.com/bigdaddyrockstar;
page 22, ©iStockphoto.com/LajosRepasi; page 25, ©iStockphoto.com/
mandygodbehear; page 26, ©NinaMalyna, used under license from
Shutterstock, Inc.

Library of Congress Cataloging-in-Publication Data
Pascaretti, Vicki.
  Super smart information strategies. Team up online / by Vicki Pascaretti
and Sara Wilkie.
      p. cm.—(Information explorer)
  Includes bibliographical references and index.
  ISBN-13: 978-1-60279-644-7   ISBN-10: 1-60279-644-0 (lib.bdg.)
  ISBN-13: 978-1-60279-652-2   ISBN-10: 1-60279-652-1 (pbk.)
  1. Internet research—Juvenile literature. 2. Research teams—Juvenile
literature. 3. Wikis (Computer science)—Juvenile literature. I. Wilkie,
Sara. II. Title. III. Title: Team up online. IV. Series.
  ZA4228.P38 2010
  025.042—dc22   2009027082

Cherry Lake Publishing would like to acknowledge the work
of The Partnership for 21st Century Skills. Please visit
www.21stcenturyskills.org for more information.

Printed in the United States of America
Corporate Graphics Inc.
January 2010
CLSP06

Table of Contents

CHAPTER ONE
It's All About Teamwork!

Have you ever been on a soccer or dance team? Have you ever been assigned a group project for school? If so, you know how important it is to work together. Have you ever teamed up online? There are many tools that help you work with others on the Web. It's time to explore teaming up online!

Teamwork is important in sports. It is just as important for school group projects.

4

Collaborating online involves working with others through the use of computers and the Internet. There are many ways to link up online. With the help of your parents, teachers, or a media specialist, you can make a wiki or use a social networking site. You can post text to a blog, too.

Why team up online? There are many advantages. You can work on the same activity at the same time as your friends. But you can all work from different places and computers. You can all read different online sources. You will be able to explore many more ideas than one person could on her own. And you aren't limited to working with friends and classmates. You can even work with students from around the world.

Would you enjoy working with students who live in another country? Working online can make that happen!

Consider THIS

As a team, you may not always agree. So what makes a team successful? Respecting everyone's opinion is one aspect. Having a positive attitude is important, too. All group members should feel comfortable sharing their ideas and trust that the others will support them. Try to include parts of everyone's ideas in a project. Be careful about judging another person's work. A good team also allows everyone to take the lead from time to time. And everyone should complete the work assigned to him or her. Remember that as a team, you are really a network of learners. By working together, you'll all learn more!

There are sites on the Internet that allow you to work with others to solve puzzles, research information for class projects, and much more. These are fantastic ways to learn from others and share what you know, too.

Always stay safe online. Some sites may ask you for private information before allowing you to access them. Private information includes personal facts about you. They should never be shared on the Internet. When in doubt, ask an adult to help you figure out if it is a good idea to post something on the Web. Remember, posting something on the Internet means others can see what you write.

stop, don't write
in the book!

TRY THIS!

Take a look at this list of information.
For each item you should never share
online, put a checkmark in the "Is
This Private?" column. Then put a
checkmark in the "OK to Share"
column next to each item you can
share with others online.

Information	Is This Private?	OK to Share
Your last name		
Your address		
Your phone number		
Your school's name or address		
Your password		
Pictures of yourself		
Your nickname		
The weather or climate where you live		
The name of your goldfish		
Your favorite flavor of ice cream		
What you think or know about a particular topic		
Your username		
Your email address		

Did you put checkmarks for privacy next
to the first six items on the list? These
are all things that should never be
shared online. The last seven items on
the list are things that are usually okay
to share with others online.

Safety
Manners
Adult Supervison
Responsibility
Teamwork

There are some basic ideas to keep in mind when working online: safety, manners, adult supervision, responsibility, and teamwork. To help you remember them, take the first letter of each idea to form a word: **SMART**.

We know that our online safety is important. But you should always remember your manners, too.

Be respectful of others and their opinions. Always use polite language online. Having manners also means remembering to give credit to the original author when sharing other people's work.

A trusted adult is the best partner when working on the Internet. Be sure to ask your parents, a media specialist, a teacher, or another adult before logging on to the Internet to collaborate with peers. Adult supervision is important whenever you are ready to explore any Web activity.

You are responsible for everything you post. No exceptions! Many others will be able to read what you write. It is your responsibility to be sure that your information is accurate. It is also important for you to report inappropriate content to an adult right away.

You know by now that teamwork is important. Help others improve their skills and efforts on a group project by offering feedback. Be specific and give details about what you observe and suggestions for improvement. Word your thoughts in positive ways. And if you don't agree about something, be polite.

When you politely disagree, you use kind words to express why you do not agree with something another group member has posted.

Did you Know this?

Remember that your online teammates will often not be able to see your face. They can't hear the tone of your voice, either. This can make it easy for others to misunderstand your message. Always write as clearly and politely as possible.

In this book, you will learn how to build a collaborative, digital space and invite friends to work with you on many explorations. A collaborative, digital space is a place where people can work together online to build a shared understanding of something. No matter how far away people are, they can still work together using digital tools. There are many options. We will focus on the use of wikis. Wikis are collections of Web pages that allow users to edit, change, and add information.

Taking care of a wiki is like taking care of a garden. A real garden requires planting, watering, weeding, and attention to grow. So does your wiki! Here are some basic steps for caring for your wiki:

- Plant—post your first thoughts on the wiki page
- Dig—research to uncover more information
- Water—add images, more information, and new resources, or make connections to something new
- Weed—correct spelling errors and incorrect information and remove inappropriate content
- Ponder—be a reflective learner by taking the time to think about how and what you've learned

CHAPTER TWO
Plant

It's time to create a wiki. Ask a parent, teacher, or media specialist to help you set up your first wiki. Think about a topic for your wiki page. Do you love baseball? Mint chocolate chip ice cream? Frogs? Be creative with your idea.

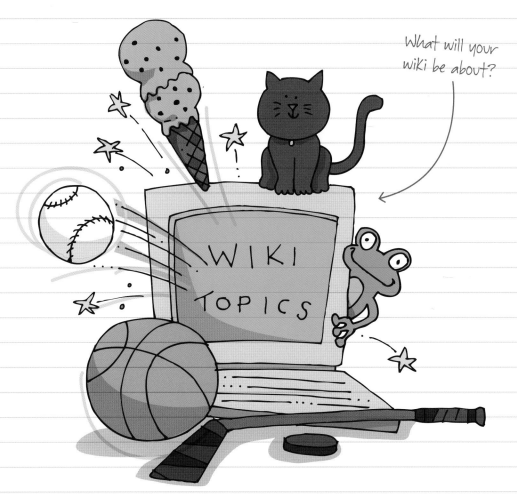

What will your wiki be about?

TRY THIS!

Once you have a topic for your wiki, follow these steps:

1. Create a new page on a wiki site. The specific steps to follow may be slightly different depending on which site you choose.

2. Give your wiki page a title that describes your topic.

3. Once you've created the page, click the edit button.

4. Add the headings "I Know . . ." and "I Wonder . . ."

5. Post three things you know about your topic under the "I Know . . ." heading.

6. Post three things you are curious about or don't know about your topic under the "I Wonder . . ." heading.

7. Ask an adult to help you invite a few friends to your new page. Remind your friends to ask an adult before accepting your invitation!

8. Have your friends add what they know and wonder about your topic under each heading on your page.

9. Ask your friends to add a new page about their own topic of interest. They should create "I Know . . ." and "I Wonder . . ." headings for their pages, too.

10. Finally, ask everyone to post what they know and wonder about each topic on one another's pages.

Once you've planted your wiki page, you're ready to garden! Remember that ways to garden a wiki include digging, weeding, and watering.

Weeding means correcting spelling errors or incorrect information. It also involves removing any inappropriate or unrelated content. Think of a wiki about frogs. If you discover a sentence about toads, you might suggest removing that sentence. When weeding another person's wiki page, the most polite move is to leave your editing suggestions in the discussion area of the wiki. The discussion tab is often found near the top of the page. Do not just delete someone else's work.

It is important to edit wikis to be sure they are accurate.

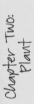

Adding more information to your wiki can make it better and more helpful to those who read it.

Watering means adding something new or related to the topic. You might add more text and information, images, or connections to other ideas. Imagine a wiki about horses. You might add a link to information about the Kentucky Horse Park. When adding something to a wiki, it's important to include your resource. That way, others will know where you found the information. Images are great additions to many wikis. Include pictures on your wiki page that you've drawn and scanned, taken with a camera, or downloaded. If you use images taken from Web sites, make sure you give credit to those sites. Paste the Web address or URL underneath the image on your wiki page. Weeding and watering strengthen and improve the content of a wiki page.

In order to grow as a learner, it helps to do some self-assessment. Pondering, or thinking carefully, helps you reflect on your own ideas and experiences. Consider what you've learned from this chapter and how you learned it. How can the processes of weeding or watering change the information you plant? Can they improve your wiki page? Now think about wikis in general. What do you like about wikis as learning tools? What do you dislike about them?

You can keep a record of your thoughts and answers to these "ponder" questions in the discussion area of your wiki page. Try repeating the reflection process after each activity. Pondering pays off!

What did you just learn about wiki pages? Ponder it!

Wiki Gardener

CHAPTER THREE
Dig

It is time for you and some friends to select another topic to explore! This time, you will develop the content of your wiki as a group. What will you all decide to investigate further? To find out, your team must reach a consensus.

A consensus is a shared agreement among the members of a team. A good team works together to reach an agreement about the topic it will investigate. You might want to explore your own topic. But try to keep an open mind. Respect other viewpoints and try to find the benefits of learning about something different.

⌐ A group that works well together can accomplish a lot!

TRY THIS!

Certain steps can help you decide which topic to explore as a group. Make a list of the pros and cons—the advantages and disadvantages—of each possible topic. Use the discussion tab or link on a new wiki page to share your lists of pros and cons with your friends. This process will help keep everyone's thoughts organized and focused on the particular topics. What will your team decide to research?

Consider this . . . . . .

What skills did you use to reach a consensus? Think about those. How will these same skills help you become a better teammate in general?

⌐Do you like to search for books at the library?

Once your team has decided on a topic, come up with several "I Wonder . . ." questions to research. Add them to the wiki. Make sure everyone is assigned an equal number of questions to research.

Now it's time to research and dig deep for information about your assigned topic. Look for interesting facts and details about the topic. Search for a variety of sources: Web sites, encyclopedia articles, online databases, and books are just a few options. How can you tell if you can trust the information in a resource? Ask yourself some questions. When was the book or article published? You may not want to use very old sources. Is the author an expert on the topic? Be extra careful online. Who created or supports the Web site? Good sources are often sites that end in .edu and .gov. When was it updated? Your goal is to find current, reliable sources.

Gathering research can be tiring. But it also is very rewarding once you find the correct information. A great tip is to try and triangulate your data. This means finding the same information in three different sources. The process helps you dig deep and be sure that your information is accurate and reliable.

Plant your answers on the wiki after you finish researching. Make sure you put your answers in your own words and give credit to your sources. Think about adding video and audio clips, links, resources, and examples to support your answers.

If you find the same information in three different sources, that information is probably correct.

TRY THIS!

Find at least three different resources that have the same information about specific aspects of your topic. Include these resources with your wiki posts.

Now take a moment to ponder your work up to this point. Create a ponder post in the discussion area of your wiki and use "Digging" as the subject. Answer each of the following questions:

- Which research questions could you answer by simply finding facts?
- Which questions required you to gather more information to find a pattern or answer?
- What did finding several resources with the same information tell you?
- Why is it important to include your resources with your answers?
- How did adding video or audio clips, links, or examples affect your wiki?
- Look at the broad topics on the home page of your subject directory. Where would you most likely find information connected to your keywords?
- Search by keyword or drill down. Give it a try!

CHAPTER FOUR
Garden

Now that you've planted your collaborative wiki page, you're ready to do some more gardening! Remember that gardening a wiki means you can dig, weed, or water the information on the pages. Work with your team to decide which sections each member will garden. You should not garden the same "I Wonder . . ." answers that you've posted. Also, be sure that each "I Wonder . . ." answer has a gardener. Use your SMART points (safety, manners, adult supervision, responsibility, and teamwork) to guide you through the process.

Be SMART about gardening your wiki!

TRY THIS!

Using the T-factor (teamwork) in our SMART guide, offer positive, specific, and polite feedback to two other teammates. Is an idea worded in a confusing way? Do you spot an incorrect fact? Use the discussion tab to post your feedback. Use your teammate's first name as the subject. See how many different forms of sources you can use to support your feedback. Web sites, images, and articles are some options.

Now take a moment to ponder this activity. Use "Gardening" as the subject in your discussion area and answer each of the following questions.

- What could be gained from having more than one person garden a page?
- Which of the SMART steps was the easiest for you? Why?
- Which SMART steps did your teammates use? How did they help improve your wiki?

You and your group now have an opportunity to plan a get-together by teaming up online. Create a new wiki page with "Garden Party" as your title. Think of all the strategies and lessons you've learned from growing your wiki garden. What will be important for you to remember as you work with your team to plan and organize this party?

Party time!

Garden Party

TRY THIS!

As you plan your party, remember to keep these steps in mind:

1. Ask an adult to supervise the planning of the party and the actual party.
2. Come up with a theme for the party that relates to the topic of your collaborative wiki. Was your wiki about volleyball? Have a volleyball-themed party!
3. Use the new wiki page to decide with your team on a time and a place for the party. Make sure everyone's parents or guardians approve of the place. You can also use the wiki to create a list of supplies for the party and to decide who will bring which supplies.

You won't need to mail party invitations if you invite friends online.

Use the wiki to invite friends to your party and encourage them to participate on your wiki page. After the get-together, create an "After Party" subject in the discussion area of the wiki. Invite your guests to offer feedback on your party.

It is important for you and your group to think about some goals for improving your SMART skills. Do you need to work on your online manners? Could you be a better team player? What connections can you draw between the goals set by each teammate? Are there common issues that everyone can work to improve?

Working together can be fun when everyone is a good team player.

CHAPTER FIVE

Ponder

Many gardeners enjoy sitting back and reflecting on the results of their hard work. You should do the same, wiki gardeners!

How does a gardener know she has done a good job?

TRY THIS!

Think about how far you and your wikis have come. Use the discussion tab on your collaborative wiki to answer the following questions:

1. How has your wiki page changed since you first posted what you knew and wondered about your own topic of interest?
2. What have you learned from these changes?
3. How did working as a team help you better understand your group's topic? Has the overall process helped you learn more about working well in a group setting?
4. How might the information you planted, dug up, weeded, and watered help others who were not involved in the process?
5. What advantages are there to inviting other friends to garden your wiki pages?
6. How would this project have been different if your team had used telephones, email, or other ways to communicate? Do you think wikis are effective tools for organizing information for others to view?

As you answer these reflection questions, it is important to always think about what you have posted on the Internet. As a team, answering these questions will help you and your friends become experts at sharing information. You will learn many things as you explore ways to work together online. Remember to be SMART when teaming up online. Use this checklist to make sure you don't miss any tips:

SMART Checklist

SAFETY

☐ I did not include personal or private information.
☐ I did not include any images of myself.
☐ I told a responsible adult if I was asked to share personal or private information.

MANNERS

☐ I used polite and respectful words in my posts.
☐ I posted my work in my own words.
☐ I gave my partners opportunities to post their own work.
☐ I included my resources every time I offered feedback about someone else's work.

RESPONSIBILITY

☐ My posts are accurate and appropriate.
☐ My information is connected to my topic.
☐ My sources are dependable and accurate.
☐ I realize that I am responsible for everything I have posted.
☐ I reported any inappropriate online content to an adult right away.

Stop, don't write in the book!

ADULT SUPERVISION

☐ I asked a responsible adult for permission before accessing the Internet.

TEAMWORK

☐ I acted as one member of a larger team, sharing the lead and taking turns.

☐ I chose my words carefully.

☐ My work strengthened the work of my team. I offered specific, positive, and polite feedback.

☐ I gardened the posts of my teammates in ways that I would like to have others garden mine.

Like a garden, wikis change and grow. Aren't you excited to see how yours will develop?

Teaming up online is fun and exciting. It allows you to work with others to connect and organize information in ways that make sense to you. You'll build writing and communication skills. Working together online also helps you understand what it means to be a responsible teammate. So what are you waiting for? The possibilities are endless with online collaboration!

Glossary

blog **(BLAWG)** a Web site that has a personal, online journal with entries from its author

collaborating **(kuh-LAB-uh-ray-teeng)** working together to do something

consensus **(kuhn-SEN-suhss)** an agreement among all people in a discussion or meeting

drill down **(DRIL DOWN)** to click on subtopics in a subject directory to narrow your search results

feedback **(FEED-bak)** reactions to something or comments about something

inappropriate **(in-uh-PROH-pree-it)** not right or proper for the situation, time, or place

post **(POHST)** publish or put work or messages on a wiki, blog, or other online setup

reliable sources **(ri-LYE-uh-buhl SOR-siz)** well-researched sources of information that are written by experts, have been reviewed by other experts in the field, and are usually current, depending on the topic

self-assessment **(self-uh-SESS-muhnt)** the process of rating your progress, strengths, and weaknesses and determining points that need improvement or changes you can make

subject directory **(SUHB-jikt due-REK-tuh-ree)** a list of Web resources that is arranged by topic

triangulate **(trye-ANG-gyuh-layt)** to find three resources or sets of data with the same information to help verify facts and ideas

wiki **(WI-kee)** a Web site that allows users to add and edit content and information

Find Out More

BOOKS

Gaines, Ann Graham. *Ace Your Internet Research*. Berkeley Heights, NJ: Enslow Publishers, 2009.

Jakubiak, David J. *A Smart Kid's Guide to Internet Privacy*. New York: PowerKids Press, 2010.

WEB SITES

Class Wiki Mission Control Center

pascaretti.wikis.birmingham.k12.mi.us/

Check out some wiki pages made by students.

FEMA for Kids—Online Safety

www.fema.gov/kids/on_safety.htm

Read a list of online safety rules.

KidsHealth—Group Projects for School

kidshealth.org/kid/feeling/school/group_projects.html#

Find tips on collaborating and working well with others.

Index

About the Authors

Vicki is a facilitator in Birmingham, Michigan. She enjoys traveling and reading. She is the mother of Deanna, Bryan, and Jody, and the proud grandmother of Christopher, Cameron, Cullen, and Trey.

Sara is a learner, teacher, and teacher facilitator in Birmingham, Michigan. She is most inspired by the love and support of Steve, Courtney, Matthew, and Brennen, and truly appreciates the motivation she receives from her colleagues.